Sta
MW01714124
Nonprofit

10 Proven Steps to Creating Your First Successful Nonprofit Organization

Jerry Kershen

©2015

Table Of Contents

© Copyright 2015 by Jerry Kershen - All rights reserved.

By accepting to read this book, you understand that there is a risk of injury associated with applying the information that contains this book, either mental or physical. You hereby assume full responsibility for any and all injuries, losses and damages. The information contained in this book is for general information purposes only.

The information is provided by our company and while we endeavor to keep the information up to date and correct, we make no representations or warranties of any kind, express or implied, about the completeness, accuracy, reliability, suitability or availability with respect to the information contained on the book for any purpose. Any reliance you place on such information is therefore strictly at your own risk. We remind you that you should always consult your physician or other healthcare provider before changing your diet or starting an exercise program. You should always consult a therapist before starting mental exercises, or any kind of program related to self-help.

This document is geared towards providing exact and reliable information in regards to the topic and issue covered. The publication is sold with the idea that the publisher is not required to render accounting, officially permitted, or otherwise, qualified services. If advice is necessary, legal or professional, a practiced individual in the profession should be ordered.

From a Declaration of Principles which was accepted and approved equally by a Committee of the American Bar Association and a Committee of Publishers and Associations.

In no way is it legal to reproduce, duplicate, or transmit any part of this document in either electronic means or in printed format. Recording of this publication is strictly prohibited and any storage of this document is not allowed unless with written permission from the publisher. All rights reserved.

The information provided herein is stated to be truthful and consistent, in that any liability, in terms of inattention or otherwise, by any usage or abuse of any policies, processes, or directions contained within is the solitary and utter responsibility of the recipient reader. Under no circumstances will any legal responsibility or blame be held against the publisher for any reparation, damages, or monetary loss due to the information herein, either directly or indirectly.

Respective authors own all copyrights not held by the publisher.

The information herein is offered for informational purposes solely, and is universal as so. The presentation of the information is without contract or any type of guarantee assurance.

The trademarks that are used are without any consent, and the publication of the trademark is without permission or backing by the trademark owner. All trademarks and brands within this book are for clarifying purposes only and are the owned by the owners themselves, not affiliated with this document.

INTRODUCTION

First and foremost I want to thank you for downloading the book, "Starting a Nonprofit: 10 Proven Steps to Creating Your First Successful Nonprofit Organization."

You already have the passion to create a nonprofit. All you need is the step by step guidance that will help you succeed. That is what you will find in this book. Come along on the journey, as this book leads you from creating your vision statement to getting your federal tax-exempt certification. Learn all the pitfalls, and tips on areas where you really must concentrate on opening your first successful nonprofit.

Thanks again for downloading this book, I hope you enjoy it!

Become Inspired

There are over 29 different types of organizations that can qualify for nonprofit status. The largest group of these nonprofits, over 35 percent, are in the human resource area. About 17 percent of these organizations help educate people. Another 13 percent work to help people take care of medical needs. Almost 12 percent of nonprofits work to benefit society. The remainders are religious organizations, those who serve animals and the environment, and those who operate in the area of international and foreign affairs.

If the money generated by nonprofits were a world economy, it would be the 16th-largest economy in the world, according to the National Council of Nonprofits. According to the United States Bureau of Labor Statistics, about 10.2 percent of all Americans are paid by a nonprofit.

There are disadvantages and advantages of forming a nonprofit organization. Cost of legal help is one of the major disadvantages of forming and incorporating a nonprofit. One way to overcome this disadvantage is that many people find that they can do much of the legal work themselves; while other nonprofits find that they must hire other professional help like an accountant, on a regular basis.

The founders of a nonprofit often find themselves working many hours each week. Often they are not paid for all of the hours that they put into the nonprofit. This can lead to burn out and the founders' attitude turning sour. This attitude can even discourage others who are working on the project.

The government has very stringent rules on how a nonprofit can operate. Some people find that these rules are way too confining for what they hope to accomplish. Therefore, they choose to not go through the process. Many of these people find other ways to accomplish the same tasks.

There are, however, many advantages to forming a nonprofit. The first benefit that almost everyone is aware of is that nonprofits do not pay many taxes. This can be a huge benefit because the average corporation pays over 12 percent in corporate taxes each year. Almost all nonprofits are eligible to not pay state taxes either. The exact rules concerning taxes that nonprofits have to pay are constantly changing and vary greatly by location.

The streams of income may increase when you form a nonprofit .For example; many public and private foundations are required by their bylaws to give money only to nonprofits. Additionally, many people are more likely to give money to nonprofits, because they may be able to write the donation off of their taxes.

Many people worry about their personal liability when they operate a company. The good news is that once a nonprofit is established, most people cannot be held personally liable for what happens with the nonprofit. This protection usually extends to board members and employees conducting the nonprofit's business.

Most people who form a nonprofit sincerely hope that the nonprofit outlives them. This is known as "organizational perpetuity". Additionally, people are more likely to donate when they know that the organization will go on for a long time.

Once the organization becomes big enough to have employees, then being a nonprofit allows employees to receive benefits including health and life insurance.

Being a nonprofit forces the organization to be organized. Some of the things that the nonprofit will need to have in place include a mission statement, procedures for delegating authority, and rules for electing board members.

There are other advantages that may vary by the organization. Generally, nonprofits can get lower postal rates for "snail mail". Some radio and television stations offer free advertising to nonprofits.

If you have decided that creating a nonprofit is right for you and your organization, then this guide answers many questions. This book will guide you step-by-step through many of the procedures that need to be completed.

Before you begin, spend some time daydreaming about what the organization can become. There is lots of work ahead and you may need the daydreams to carry you through the work ahead.

Step 1: Writing Nonprofit Vision and Mission Statements

Before you create a mission statement, it is vital to create a vision statement. The vision statement is the reason that the nonprofit exists. For example, an animal shelter may have the mission of helping animals in a particular geographical area. The vision statement should remind anyone reading or hearing the statement of what is possible. Vision statements should stand as the inspiration behind an organization and serve as a map to get the nonprofit's job accomplished. A vision statement should serve as a guide to make sure that the organization is moving in the right direction.

In order to write the vision statement, start by assembling a group of individuals who are committed to achieving the same goal. Then, allow them to brainstorm ideas. In the beginning, make sure that everyone understands that they are not to pass judgment on anyone's idea. Free sharing of ideas produces stronger vision statements.

Vision statements should be kept short. In most cases, the statement should be less than two sentences. It helps if the statement is catchy. Eliminate all unnecessary words. If possible, create the vision statement and then let a few days pass by. Return to the vision statement and make sure that it still makes sense.

Now that you have created the vision statement, the mission statement should further explain that vision statement. Again, when you are writing the mission statement it is important to seek input from others who are interested in the activity.

The mission statement should define how the organization plans to carry out their vision statement. It should clearly state what makes the organization unique from other nonprofits. The mission statement should be clear and not contain any jargon. One of the primary reasons that this is so important is that you will want to share the mission statement with prospective donors. If the mission statement is full of jargon, those donors may not understand your statement and choose to give another nonprofit the funds that you need to operate.

The nonprofit mission statement must answer three fundamental questions. The first of these questions is what are the needs that the nonprofit is being formed to address. The answer should be as unique as the organization.

The second question that the mission statement must address is what the organization will be doing to address those needs. The answer to this question should also be very unique. It is important that input into this question be solicited from many different people. Talk to others who are already working in nonprofits similar to yours, within the local community. This is to make sure that you are not duplicating services unless the need that duplication exists is helpful. You may also want to email people who are active in similar organizations in other communities to see what they are doing. You need to talk to people that are interested in the cause to see what they think the nonprofit needs to be doing. Do not overlook the importance of talking to people that the organization exists to serve to solicit their ideas.

The third question that the mission statement should address is what beliefs or values are going to guide the nonprofit. These values are usually expressed in the terms of active adjectives that describe how employees and volunteers will act when representing the nonprofit.

Now that you have some basic ideas, it is time to put it all together. The mission statement should inspire people that are going to be active in the nonprofit. This includes board members, employees and those served by the nonprofit. If the mission statement is not motivational, then it needs to be adjusted. The mission statement should not be long. In fact, it should be so short that those who are part of the nonprofit can recite it from memory.

Review the mission statement on a regular basis. It is a *living* document that needs to be changed as the nonprofit's purposes are more clearly defined. This process must continue for the life of the nonprofit.

As an example, the American Heart Association was formed in 1915 and one of its first acts of business was to create a mission statement. That statement has been changed very few times since then. Yet, the association sets aside a specific time to examine the mission statement each year to make sure that it remains relevant.

As mentioned earlier, the first step in creating a nonprofit should be to create a vision statement followed by a mission statement. These statements should serve as the guiding force behind an organization. Therefore, it is important to solicit answers to key questions from many different groups. Again, both should be kept short and not filled with jargon.

The mission statement is one of the most important statements that a nonprofit can create. Creating a compelling mission statement does many things for your organization. It allows the nonprofit to clarify its purpose. It also helps to energize your volunteer base and get board members excited. It helps you solicit funds from foundations. Perhaps, most importantly for the new nonprofit, it helps the Internal Revenue Service (IRS) determine your purpose and approve your application for nonprofit status more quickly.

STEP 2: CHOOSE THE ORGANIZATIONAL TYPE

Before you can begin to make plans to become a nonprofit in the United States, you must determine what classification the nonprofit falls under according to the Internal Revenue Service. The Internal Revenue Service recognizes many different types of nonprofits.

Social welfare nonprofits must have the express purpose of bettering the lives of the people that they serve. These organizations, known as 501(c)4s, must serve all members of the community. While they are allowed to participate in some political lobbying on behalf of all members of the community, they must not support a particular candidate. Common examples of social welfare organizations include organizations focused on improving society and on bettering individual communities.

Agriculture and horticulture organizations are tax-exempt nonprofits focused on helping farmers, ranchers, fisherman, and ornamental growers. Common activities that these nonprofits may participate in include: determining which animals are pure, promoting their product to the consumer, and promoting research within their particular area of interest.

Labor organizations are another type of nonprofit. Their purpose is to promote and bargain for rights of workers within a particular company.

Business leagues, commonly called trade associations, are another type of nonprofit. These nonprofits are built to promote common interests of people in a particular industry. Generally, they cannot perform activities, such as sales, that people normally do to make a profit.

Social clubs are also a type of nonprofits. These clubs must have the express purpose of connecting members with each other. Additionally, membership to the club must be limited. No profits from these clubs can benefit an individual or a group of individuals.

Fraternal societies are another type of nonprofit. The members of these nonprofits are often organized into lodges. All members of these nonprofits must have a common interest or tie. Additionally, fraternal societies must pay benefits such as accident, life or health to its members.

Employee benefit associations are not used very much anymore but they are still a type of a nonprofit. The idea behind these organizations is that everyone pays dues that benefit all members. In particular, they were often used to help members receive medical care.

Veteran organizations are groups of veterans who have banded together to form a unit. These units can also include the spouse or children of veterans. The key to being a nonprofit tax-exempt veteran organization is that all members must have completed United States military service.

Public charities are one of the most popular types of nonprofits. These organizations must have an active fundraising component. Churches and hospitals are two common types of public charities.

Private foundations are also a type of nonprofit. Unlike public charities, these organizations usually have one main donor who provides the money for the foundation.

Political organizations are yet another type of nonprofit. These organizations may form to support a particular candidate. They may also form to support a particular point of view.

After a nonprofit has been created, it is essential that the nonprofit decide which type of association they are going to be because it determines their ability to get funding and not have to pay taxes.

STEP 3: NAME THE NONPROFIT

Naming a nonprofit can be fun, but it can also be quite frustrating if done improperly. It is vital to come up with a name that represents your nonprofit and that you can trademark. While an exciting step, many people find it much more complicated than naming their first-born child.

Come up with a name for your nonprofit by brainstorming ideas with a group of people. You can do this at the same meeting where you create your vision and mission statement or at a separate meeting. Suggest that everyone come to the meeting with a list of possible names. Then, allow everyone to share those names. Some leaders even find it helpful to list the names on a board so everyone can see them.

The best names often come from unusual sources, so make sure that you have others who are committed, help you name the nonprofit.

During this stage, it is important to value everyone's idea. It is not only important so that you get the best names, but it establishes the underlying tone of respect for people within your nonprofit.

Experts suggest that the best names are those that convey the mission of the organization. The best names are also short and express the values of the organization. They often incorporate active verbs, but always convey a concrete idea.

Once a list of possible names has been created, then start narrowing down the list. Have someone search for each name to see if anyone has already come up with the idea. Trademarking a name is not possible if someone is already using it. Trademarking the name is essential when you go to file paperwork to become a tax-exempt organization. Additionally, completing this step usually cuts the list of possible names in about half, so there will be less discussion on which name is best.

Now take favorite names and see if the domain is available on the Go Daddy website (www.godaddy.com) or other website which registers domains. At some point your organization will want a website, and if the nonprofit's name is already taken, then that can become a problem. Remember that most nonprofit website addresses end in. org.

The next step is to check the name with the United States Patent and Trademark Office (www.uspto.gov/). You can use their easy-to-use online database to see if the name is already trademarked. If it is, then choose a different name. That is why you need to have several choices available at this point.

Now that you have an even shorter list, it is time to contact the Secretary of State or a similar office in the state where the nonprofit will operate. In most states, this is a free service. The procedure varies by state, but usually you will have to submit a form that can be found on the state's website. Some states allow you to call the state and see if a name is available for a nominal charge.

Once you have found a name that is great for your nonprofit and that can be trademarked, then go back to Go Daddy website (www.godaddy.com) and claim that domain. This prevents anyone else from using that website. With hundreds of people trying to work through the process every day, it is quite possible that someone else has come up with the idea.

The next step is to select a trademark format. In this area, your nonprofit has three different choices. You can choose to trademark it using just standard characters. While a little boring, this method is quick and efficient. You can also choose to trademark your name using a stylized format, sometimes called a design format. In this format, you choose to incorporate a logo type trademark name. Finally, you can choose to incorporate a sound mark, which is the trademark in an audible format.

Now, head back to the United States Patent and Trademark Office website (www.uspto.gov/) website and seek a trademark on that name. Once the office approves your paperwork, then you can begin using that name. While some people choose to work with a professional during the naming process, it is a process that most nonprofit leaders can accomplish on their own, protecting the limited resources of startup nonprofits.

STEP 4: CHOOSE A BOARD OF DIRECTORS

Nonprofits are required to have a board of directors. These individuals should share your vision for what the nonprofit can become over the course of its life. These individuals are leaders of the nonprofit, but should not, in most cases be employees of the nonprofit.

Many nonprofits try to put too many people on their boards. In all cases, the number of board members should be an odd number so that no vote can end in a tie. Generally, if the board is supposed to oversee the operations of a nonprofit on a regular basis, then a smaller board is desired. Often the number of directors is determined by the strategic priorities of the nonprofit so that each member oversees one area.

There are four basic responsibilities of a board member. The government considers these responsibilities so important that they hold board member's legally responsible for seeing that the nonprofit upholds its responsibility to the public.

The first duty of the board is to define the nonprofit's mission. The second duty is to establish priorities for the nonprofit. Then the board is responsible for creating strategies for carrying out those priorities. Finally, the board creates a plan that ensures those strategies are implemented.

There are many different ways that a leader can choose who serves on a board. In the functional approach, each board member is chosen for their skills to oversee a particular area. When choosing functional board members, it is vital, however, to make sure that the members also represent diversity within the community in regards to sex, age and other qualifying characteristics.

Another approach to choosing a board of directors is the diversification approach. Under this method, each board member is chosen because of their ethnicity, age or other qualifying characteristics. Nonprofits who employ this approach often must train the board of directors in the role that they want the person to fulfill.

Yet, another approach is the representative approach. Under this approach, each board member is selected to represent a particular area. This approach often works well when different organizations are joining together to form the nonprofit with each group having one member on the board of directors. Other times, this approach works well when the nonprofit wants to ensure that all geographical areas receive equal representation.

While many beginning nonprofits try to use the passion approach, this approach is often not the best approach because it does not offer enough diversity in the board of directors. People who are passionate about the nonprofit's cause may also mean extremely heated board meetings.

Some states have implemented rules governing the number of people that serve on boards. In almost all cases, at least three members are required. Therefore, it is essential to check applicable state laws before determining the exact composition of your board.

If you discover that many people want to serve on the board of directors, then consider dividing the work of the board into different committees and creating a top board.

There are many advantages to using this technique. You may find that your board of directors starts to develop other interests. Therefore, some people may not be willing to work with the nonprofit for the long term.

Especially in the beginning, the nonprofit may find that there are numerous complex issues that must be studied and discussed. Dividing this work among many different committees often allows people to feel like they are making an important contribution with their limited amount of time.

Members of the board of directors have their own set of skills. Dividing the work into committees allows people to use their talents in the area where they feel strongest without having to commit to an area where they do not have the skill set. At the same time, encouraging people that may have an interest, but do not yet have the skills, encourages people to learn those skills.

The best board members are often very passionate about issues. Dividing the board into smaller groups allows individuals to share their passionate opinions without tying up the time for people that are not as passionate about a particular interest. This can be especially helpful when finances are involved, because the finance committee can keep a tighter control over the money without everyone having an input into the discussion. Then, each committee can give a report back to the entire board of directors.

Sometimes people are intimidated when they are asked to join a large group. Some people feel that if there are so many people working on an issue, that their help is not really needed. Inviting new people to smaller committee meetings has been shown to be effective in encouraging new people to take an active role.

The most qualified board members often have a limited amount of time that they can give to a nonprofit. Using committees allows that person to know when their input is especially needed. Therefore, the board member may feel more valued and be likely to be more engaged with the nonprofit.

Committees also allow new people to take on leadership responsibilities sooner. Often times all the individual needs is the chance to become involved and a little training from more experienced people to become a real asset to the board. Committees are a great way to get people to connect with each other on a social level, which encourages people to stick with the nonprofit over a longer period.

Committees also allow people to connect at a deeper emotional level with the organization. One of the major jobs of any new nonprofit is raising funds. When people are more emotionally attached to an issue, they are more likely to raise that money.

Generally, by this point, the board should have elected leaders to keep the meetings organized and aid the meetings in running smoothly. Various state laws determine what positions must be in place, and boards often expand elected positions on a board beyond the scope of the state laws.

Generally, each board of directors must have a *chair*. This individual is responsible for leading meetings.

Additionally, this individual is responsible for preparing board agendas, and seeing that board resolutions are followed. They can be very instrumental in seeing that the right board committees are formed.

It is also a great idea to have a *vice-chair*. This individual can then assume the position of the chair if something happens to the chair. This person is to assist the chair in any duties that the chair assigns. Additionally, if committees are formed, then this individual often heads those committees.

Most states require that nonprofits also have a *treasurer*. This person is ultimately responsible for seeing that financial reports are prepared for other board members to review. They should be very familiar with any state laws that must be followed so that the nonprofit stays out of financial difficulties. The individual should be responsible for preparing the annual audit or ensuring that the employee completing this task gets it done correctly. As larger board of directors are divided into smaller committees, this person often serves on special committees such as fundraising committees.

At a minimum, most board of directors should also have a *secretary*. The responsibility of this person is to be a keeper of board minutes and materials. The person should also be responsible for sending out notices of board meetings. Working alongside the chairperson, this person should ensure that all meetings are announced in concordance with state laws.

Each nonprofit must choose a board of directors following state laws. The minimum amount of people needed is usually three. There are definite advantages to limiting the number of people on a board. In almost all cases the board should come from a variety of backgrounds and have diverse skillsets. If the board becomes too large, then consider breaking it down into committees and forming a top board with each committee reporting to that board. A board of directors needs to follow state guidelines ensuring they have the required number of official positions. Additionally, many committees choose to follow these guidelines to ensure that they function smoothly.

STEP 5: CREATE ARTICLES OF INCORPORATION

Your next step is to get your articles of incorporation from the appropriate state office. While the form itself is self-explanatory in most cases, using it as a guide to set up your nonprofit allows you to make important decisions about your nonprofit.

There are many reasons that your new nonprofit needs to take this important step. If you plan on doing any fundraising and spending the money to help others, then you need to incorporate so that you do not have to pay taxes on that money. This, of course, allows the money to go further.

The second reason that you need to incorporate is that you may want to apply for grant money. If you plan on seeking donations from the public, then you need to become a tax-exempt organization, so that donors are more likely to give. In order to become a tax-exempt organization, the nonprofit must be incorporated.

Incorporating also gives you, your board of directors, and your members, freedom from personal liability should something go wrong. If you think that the nonprofit may need legal help at some point, incorporating helps a volunteer or employee in court.

Additionally, incorporating also allows you to receive special postage rates. Depending on your state, incorporating as a nonprofit means you pay no, or lower, property taxes.

Filling out the forms is usually quite simple. In most cases, the first blank is for the name of your organization. That is part of the reason that the Articles of Incorporation should be completed after the name has been trademarked.

Article II usually requires that you state that the nonprofit will be perpetual. In some states, you must declare the type of nonprofit you are forming in this section. For that reason, leaders must decide on the type of organization that best meets their needs before incorporating. Highly recommended wording for the first section of the Articles of Incorporation can be found at Form1023.org.

Article III or the article that asks you to state the mission of your nonprofit is arguably the most important article in the Articles of Incorporation. It is this section that the Internal Revenue agent will specifically look at to determine the purpose of your organization and grant or deny its tax-exempt status.

Start this section by including your mission statement. That is why it was so important that you concentrated on producing a good mission statement earlier. You can just write it down word for word in this section of the document.

Article III should also include a statement that you understand the requirements of being tax-exempt. It should state that the nonprofit has been expressly organized for:

Charitable purposes

Educational purposes

Literary purposes

National or international amateur sports competitions

Public safety testing

Religious purposes

Scientific purposes

This portion of the Articles of Incorporation must also state that money from the nonprofit will not enrich any individual's life, except in exchange for services and that those payments will be reasonable. Therefore, you should make sure to put in this article that the money raised by the nonprofit will not benefit: the creator or his or her relatives, any organizational shareholders or people that they have delegated authority to, or any private interests connected to any person within the nonprofit.

Unfortunately, over 50 percent of all nonprofits fail. Therefore, you must state in this article that any money left over after if the nonprofit fails will go to another nonprofit that has similar goals. It is not necessary however, to state the exact organization that the money will go to, but just that no individual will benefit from the nonprofit failing.

The next article simply gives the name of a person who is an agent of the corporation. In many cases, this is the creator of the nonprofit or a leader within the organization. If you are using an attorney to help you with the Articles of Incorporation, then you can use the attorney's address. Regardless, the address must be a street address and not a post office box. In other cases, the names, addresses and titles of the board of directors is listed in this part of the Articles of Incorporation.

Read your Articles of Incorporation. Some states combine this area into one, while others leave the person of contact and the directors as two separate areas. Even if you are only required by your state to list one board of directors, it is the best practice to list more than one. That way, when the IRS goes to look at the information that you are submitting, you are showing that there is community support behind the project. The IRS takes this as an important clue to see if they should approve your application for tax-exempt status.

The next area on the Articles of Incorporation is to list the incorporator. This is often just a relist of the information that you listed in the last section. Again, it is better to list at least three names in this area. Make sure to use street addresses in this area as well. Post office boxes will be rejected.

Article VII on most Articles of Incorporation asks about members. Just make a statement in this area that refers the government to the bylaws. The reason is quite simple. Bylaws are easier to amend than Articles of Incorporation.

You may find one additional area on the Articles of Incorporation. This area asks you for any additional information. Unless you have a compelling reason to do so, just leave this area blank.

Now that you and your board have written your Articles of Incorporation, it is important to file them with the correct state office. Usually this is the Secretary of State, although in some cases it may be the state comptroller's office or some other office that your state has delegated. Most states require a fee to file your Articles of Incorporation. The most common problem with Articles of Incorporation is that people forget to include this fee.

Remember to give the government exactly the information that they ask for in each section. Many state websites give examples that are easy to follow just by substituting in your information. Filing your Articles of Incorporation is a big step and one that you can be very proud of taking.

Step 6 Write Conflict of Interest Policy

Before a nonprofit can continue, they need to create a Conflict of Interest policy. It is against the law for people to act on behalf of a nonprofit where a director or employee will benefit from that action. Any time this could occur, the voting member must not vote and the reason for not voting must be stated in the minutes of the meeting. The policy in particular must cover any director, any person who has the right to make business decisions for the nonprofit, and any member of a committee who may serve on the top governing board. In order to cover all bases, many nonprofits assume that it applies to everyone.

It is very important to understand that a financial interest can involve the payment of money, but it may also include gifts or favors. In other words, any way that the business in front of the nonprofit may benefit one of its members. If a person is dedicated enough to be on more than one nonprofit, and the two nonprofits have any dealings in common, then that too must be announced.

Many nonprofits find that their states provide a form for this policy with fill-in-the-blank opportunities. Nonetheless, it is vital that the entire board understand what the Conflict of Interest policy says so that they can follow it carefully.

According to the Internal Revenue Service, the purpose of this policy is to "protect this tax-exempt organization's (Organization) interest when it is contemplating entering into a transaction or arrangement that might benefit the private interest of an officer or director of the Organization, or might result in a possible excess benefit transaction. This policy is intended to supplement, but not replace, any applicable state and federal laws governing conflict of interest applicable to nonprofit and charitable organizations."

If a director, principle officer, or employee says that he or she may have a conflict of interest, then the individual must tell the meeting all of the relevant facts. After the individual has made a statement, then that person must leave the meeting. The board or committee must then decide if a conflict of interest exists.

The chairperson of the board of directors or another leader must then appoint an individual to determine if an alternative to the conflict of interests exist. This committee or person must recommend to the board if another alternative exists that is more advantageous to the nonprofit. The entire committee, minus the person who may have a conflict of interest, must decide if doing business so that it benefits the person who has the conflict of interest is in the best interest of the nonprofit. When these discussions occur, the minutes must record the name of the individual, the possible conflict of interest, and the nonprofit's findings. When the vote is held, then the minutes must reflect how each member voted.

The government takes conflict of interest problems very seriously. Therefore, your board should take any reasonable steps to avoid problems in this area. If a problem is discovered, the first step that the nonprofit should take is to confront the individual and ask for an explanation. If the nonprofit feels that the member does not immediately correct the situation, then the member must be disciplined. Usually this involves returning at least 20 percent of the money received or a gift to the nonprofit. In some cases, however, all of the funds must be returned to the nonprofit.

Each director, principle officer and employee of the nonprofit must annually sign a Conflict of Interest statement. These statements must be retained by the nonprofit.

Step 7 Create a Website

Now you should create your nonprofit website. Not only will potential donors use this website to learn more about your organization, but so will the IRS. You need the website up and running properly before you file your request to become a tax-exempt organization with the IRS.

If you have not already done so, claim your domain name from the Go Daddy website (www.godaddy.com). Then, decide on which web hosting company is right for your nonprofit. There are actually companies who give free hosting to nonprofits, so make sure to check out those options.

When choosing a web hosting company, consider if the hosting service places ads on your pages. Consider a different option, in this case, as you normally have no control over the advertising, which may not agree with what your nonprofit stands for in principle.

Consider the amount of space when choosing a web hosting company. Most sites use less than 5 megabytes, but you may want to look for a hosting company that gives you plenty of space to expand as your needs grows. If you anticipate that the site will contain many pictures of your project, then you may need even more space.

Consider how you will build the site. Many inexpensive web hosting companies only allow you to use their online site builders. While this may be very convenient to begin with, you need a company that will allow you to expand beyond this option. The reason is that these sites often look very amateurish.

The more types of files that you can upload to the site the better. Some companies limit you to HTML and GIF/JPG files. If you anticipate that your nonprofit may want to share software on the site, then this can be very limiting.

Web hosting companies have different levels of reliability and speed. This should be one of the biggest factors in choosing a web hosting company. If a potential donor is looking for your site and your site is down, you have likely missed the opportunity to get that donation. Likewise, if a site loads slowly, potential donors often view this as a sign of a low-class nonprofit and move on.

Check out the amount of bandwidth that you are allowed to use. Even web hosting companies that claim to offer unlimited bandwidth often define it further in the fine print. Therefore, it is not really unlimited.

Often combined with web hosting bandwidth offers is the amount of available disk space. Generally, your nonprofit will need less than 20 megabytes of disk space unless you plan to host videos directly on the site.

Make sure that you can get technical support 24 hours a day, 7 days a week. As you already know, things will go wrong at the most inopportune time. Therefore, choose a web hosting company that offers unlimited technical support at all times.

Look at the email programs that are available from the web hosting company. The web hosting company should offer you the chance to have multiple email addresses with your nonprofit's name at the end. This gives you a much more professional appearance when emailing people.

Now that you have chosen your web hosting company, you will need to design a great site. Ensure that updates are easy. It is important to create a professional website that your current staff and volunteers can use. If you make it too complicated, everyone will avoid using it and the site will quickly grow old.

While it is possible for almost anyone to design a website assuming they are willing, if you do not have a volunteer or staff member who has experience, this is one area where you may want to hire a professional.

Many times, you can hire a professional to get your website up and running for under $200; you can then have someone take over the responsibility of keeping it up to date.

Your nonprofit should have a content strategy. Sites that are updated on a regular basis, at least three times a week, rank higher on search engines, which may be key to having your donors find you. Therefore, it is necessary to decide what you are going to post and who is going to be responsible for posting it. If this is more than your current volunteers and staff can hire, then consider working with a professional writer who can often be hired for $1 for 100 words, for example.

A website is a necessity for a nonprofit. Claim your domain name and then choose your web hosting company. Then, decide on the right content to post on the site and keep it updated on a regular basis.

STEP 8: CRAFT THE BYLAWS

Every organization needs rules and it is no different for a nonprofit. These rules are called *bylaws*. While you will hear many people say that writing bylaws is a hard job, if you have chosen the right board of directors, this job is relatively easy.

There are three things that your bylaws must cover and a few other things that you may want to cover in your bylaws. The three things that your bylaws must cover is how are directors elected, how meetings will be conducted, and the role of employees. You may also want to incorporate other roles into your bylaws.

The first section of your bylaws should state your nonprofit's trademarked name. If you envision calling the nonprofit anything else, then list them here as well.

The second section of the bylaws should be the purpose of your nonprofit. As a general rule, you can just copy your nonprofit's mission statement into this area. At the end of the mission statement, add a sentence that says you are seeking tax-exempt status, and that you may work with other organizations that have tax-exempt status. You will also want to add that you may use volunteers or offer internships to carry out the functions of your nonprofit.

The next section of the bylaws should be titled Powers. In this section state that the nonprofit may carry out any lawful acts needed to carry out the purposes of the nonprofit. Additionally, add a sentence that indicates that you may work with other organizations as needed to carry out your nonprofit's mission. Finally, add a sentence that says that you may solicit and collect funds from the public to carry out the nonprofit's mission.

Now you are ready to write the Nonprofit Status and Exempt Activities Limitations area, which is divided into three parts. The first part states your legal status to operate. This is the type of organization that you are organizing under according to the IRS. The next part lists the activities that your type of organization cannot do.

The last part of this section deals with what you plan to do if the nonprofit closes. You will want to list that you will comply with Section 501 (c) 3; that the majority of directors will choose the exact organization to receive the funds at that time. And that if the court becomes involved, the nonprofit will comply with the court's orders.

You are now ready to write the third section of your bylaws. This section deals with membership in your nonprofit. Generally, you will want three sections. The first section should say that members have no voting rights. The second section should say that board members may admit members who are non-voting affiliates. It should further state that the membership list will not be shared or sold. The final section should be that the board of directors can establish dues.

Now, state information about your board of directors. The first section should state the minimum and maximum number of directors, followed by a section that gives the board all powers except as precluded by law. The next section should set forth the terms of how long each board of director will serve. The qualifications for directions and the election procedure should be clearly spelled out. Finally, a procedure should be spelled out that tells how a director can be removed from office.

After that section, the next section should deal with meetings. The bylaws do not need to state a specific time for meetings, but needs to spell out that meetings will be conducted in accordance to your state law. The next section should spell out the policy for special meetings. Again, it is the best policy to leave this extremely vague going with special meetings can be held in accordance with state law.

The final section of the bylaws should deal with how meetings are conducted. Include a sentence that meetings must have a quorum, majority vote and who will break any tie votes. Finally, spell out how members may participate, such as phone conversations or the internet. The very last sentence should say that directors may receive no compensation for serving, but may have travel expenses covered.

Some nonprofits choose to use the bylaws to further spell out other requirements that the nonprofit needs to put in place. These policies may include setting up committees, electing officers, what each officer is expected to do, and how the financial manners of the nonprofit will be handled. Other areas that may be added include where the books and records of the nonprofit will be maintained, what the fiscal year is, a conflict of interest policy, and a nondiscrimination policy.

The last section of the bylaws should be a procedure to amend the bylaws. After meeting conduct is outlined, then the directors may skip to this section. This allows the procedure to become tax-exempt to continue while the board is nailing down the other policies that they want to include in the bylaws.

STEP 9: PREPARE THE BUDGET

There is no question that preparing your budget is one of the first and most important jobs that the board must tackle for a new nonprofit. Yet, there are so many uncertainties that many boards find it an extremely scary process. There is, however, no way to get tax-exemption without a budget and most nonprofits fail to achieve their mission without a budget. Additionally, if you are applying for government and private sector grants, chances are that you will be asked to present your budget.

The first step in creating a budget is to form a budget committee. If the board is small, then the entire board of directors may be involved in the budgeting process, especially during the first year. Before starting on a budget, it is important to set a deadline for completing it. This ensures that the nonprofit actually has a budget and that everyone has agreed. Not having a budget is one of the main reasons that over 50 percent of all new nonprofits fail.

When determining the budget, it is important to start with the small details and build forward. Starting with the overall picture and trying to build backward does not work well.

Start by considering all the places that the nonprofit is likely to receive revenue during the upcoming year. Start by considering any grants that the nonprofit is likely to receive. When evaluating which grants are possibilities, make sure to question whether your nonprofit is in a position to meet the qualifications for that grant. Investigate what auditing reports must be maintained if the nonprofit is awarded the grant. Find out if the use of the funds is restricted in anyway. Some large grants are actually detrimental to the whole organization, because individual donors no longer believe that their money matters. In particular, try to pursue those grants that allow the nonprofit to build sustainable programs.

If the nonprofit plans to offer programs to the public that the nonprofit can receive funds for, then ask what is the expected revenue from those services. Examples of this include nonprofit hospitals that charge patients and their insurance companies or nonprofit institutions of learning that charge students tuition. Another example is a nonprofit that operates a thrift store.

Another source of revenue is contributions from people who want to be part of the mission. In fact, many nonprofits receive about 73 percent of their revenue in this way, according to a recent survey by Giving U.S.A.

Consider if there are government grants that your organization may be able to qualify for, and if that is the way that the nonprofit wants to get money. Just like with private grants, make sure you understand how the money must be spent, and what records must be retained. Again, if you have limited resources, then look for programs that will allow the nonprofit to build a sustainable program.

Federated funds exist in almost every community and are often called the United Way. Consider if the nonprofit can qualify for money through federated funds and what records must be maintained.

Private, corporate and family foundations are another source where you may be able to obtain money. See if you can locate sources that align with the mission of your nonprofit.

See if there are employers in the area that will let employees direct a portion of their paycheck directly to your cause.

Add all the expected resources together. It is far better to underestimate the amount of money that is going to come in than it is to overestimate. Doing this ensures that the nonprofit has enough money to meet its goals and allows your nonprofit to adjust to emergencies that may occur. Especially during the first year, it can be very difficult to estimate all of the expenses.

Now, it is important to decide how the nonprofit needs to spend the available money. One area that almost all nonprofits will need to budget for are direct costs. These can be costs for extra staff for a fundraising event, supplies that are needed to operate the nonprofit, and money spent on marketing.

The budget may also need to contain money for capital expenses. For example, the nonprofit may need to purchase cars or trucks for employees to drive. The nonprofit may also need to purchase real estate.

A large area of expenses for many nonprofits is overhead. These bills can include salaries for employees, along with other items in their benefit package. It can also include monthly bills such as postage, internet, phone lines and rent that must be paid every month.

Budgeting can be a big chore for the new nonprofit. Many nonprofits can benefit from others who have been down the road of establishing a similar nonprofit in the past. Others can benefit from taking a look at IRS Form 990 that nonprofits must fill out with their budgets.

STEP 10: FILE IRS FORM 1023

After you have received your approved Articles of Incorporation, your next tax is to file with the IRS for your tax-exempt status. Nonprofits have two choices in which form they want to submit to the IRS. Form 1023EZ is the easiest to fill out, but is not the right form for many nonprofits. In order to consider filling out Form 1023EZ, an organization must have less than $250,000 in assets and must expect less than $50,000 in gross receipts. Additionally, the nonprofit must think that this is all they are going to have per year over the course of the next five years. Therefore, most organizations will be better off filing Form 1023, which has 11 different parts, as of 2015.

Before you start the process, the nonprofit will need an Employee Identification Number (EIN). This number is available by filling out an easy form, called Form S4, available on the Internal Revenue Service website (http://www.irs.gov/). The person completing this form will need a social security number.

The first part of Form 1023 contains the name of the nonprofit. This should be the trademarked name of the organization. The second part of part one asks for the name of an individual. It should be the same name and address that you listed on the Articles of Incorporation. Then, you will need to list an address. Post office boxes can be used on this form. The next part asks you to list the Employee Identification Number.

Now, comes the question on your fiscal year. The fiscal year and the calendar year do not have to be the same thing. The end of the fiscal year is up to you, but there are two popular options. If you plan on applying for government grants, September 30 is a good option because it is when the government ends their fiscal year. Many other nonprofits choose December 30. Many nonprofits set reports to coincide with the fiscal year. If you want the board and others to enjoy their holidays, this may not be a good option.

The seventh question again asks you for a contact. Just list the same one that you did in section two. Since you are filling out this form for the nonprofit, there is no need to list a representative and the declaration. So answer this question, no. The next question asks you if a professional helped you with the paperwork. Since you are doing it yourself, hopefully with help from your directors, the answer is again no.

The next question asks about your nonprofit website. As covered in the last chapter, this is a requirement. One of the reasons that the Internal Revenue Service is interested is that you must announce your meetings publically. Therefore, your website can be used for this purpose. Additionally, you can use the website to be transparent, which is another criterion that the IRS looks for when granting tax-exempt status.

The very next question is one where you are going to hedge a little to get out of some work right now. For now, say that you are not exempt from filing. If you find later, that you are exempt from filing, you can just file Form 990 at a later time.

The very last question in part 1 asks you if the nonprofit was incorporated outside the United States. In most cases, the answer will be no.

Thankfully, the second part is much faster to complete than the first part. The first question asks if you are a corporation. The answer is no. The second question asks if you are a limited liability company. The answer is no. The third question asks if you are an unincorporated association. Answer no if you have been following the steps in this book. The fifth question asks if you have written your bylaws. The answer should be yes. Then, you simply attach a copy of the bylaws. This is the major reason that the board may want to include the basic requirements and then move on to adding to the bylaws at a later time.

The third part of Form 1023 starts by asking you to list where in your Articles on Incorporation they can find what makes you eligible to be a tax-exempt organization.

This is why it was so important to use the language understood by the IRS. Continue on down the list of questions by listing the article and paragraph where the information can be found.

The fourth part of Form 1023 is the most important part of your paperwork. Many former IRS agents who have approved or disapproved these forms say that they read this section first. Therefore, it is vital that you be extremely bold in this area and as specific as possible. You want the IRS representative to catch your vision for what your nonprofit will be doing.

There are several questions that you can use to guide your writing. The first question that your narrative should address is what the purpose of the nonprofit is, so you can simply copy your nonprofit's mission statement and then expand on it if needed. Some people also start this part with a copy of the nonprofit's vision statement. Then, expand this opening area with lots of information about the programs that your nonprofit hopes to conduct.

The next part of your narrative should answer the question: who will be carrying out the activities. Talk about some of the qualifications of your great board members that will allow the nonprofit to succeed at carrying out the programming. Talk about how you have community support and how you plan to recruit volunteers to help you.

Then, answer the question of where in your narrative. If you are going to operate in many different locations, then state that and share some specific examples. If you are going to have an international focus even if your organization may not go there personally, then state that fact.

Now answer the question of how your nonprofit plans to accomplish its tasks. Again, be as specific as possible. Make sure that while you are talking about the different activities, that you mention how each of these activities furthers the mission of your nonprofit.

Finally, answer the question of how the nonprofit will be funded. Identify what your possible funding sources are and why you think you can get money from those sources.

Now, that you have written a rough draft, go back and reread it. Ensure that you have used as many active verbs as possible. It often helps to have a person read the narrative who has no idea about the project to make sure that it makes sense to them. Make sure to proofread it.

You are now ready to move on to the fifth part of Form 1023. This section is also one of the most important parts of your application. The reason that this part of the IRS form is essential is that the IRS is trying to catch you in lies so that they can eliminate the bad apples who are trying to start nonprofits to become rich.

Line 1A in the fifth part asks that you state the name and address of each member of the board. Then, you must list the compensation or proposed compensation for each individual. If any members of your board are married to each other, they only count as one entry. If the person receives no compensation, then make sure to state that fact.

Pay very careful attention to the wording of parts b and c of this question. The IRS wants to see if you are paying attention. Parts b and c asks about the compensation of your five highest-paid employees. You should attach a spreadsheet here where the first column is each person's name. The second column is the person's title, the third column is the mailing address, the fourth column is the number of hours that each person works and the last column is the compensation. Since you are honest, you will have no trouble listing these people. Dishonest people often foul up here and list members of the board without having listed the compensation in the first answer. Therefore, make sure that they agree completely. Then on line 3a, you must state if any employees are related to any board members.

Then, make sure that you answer yes to every question in item four. The fifth question asks about your conflict of interest policy. Simply attach your conflict of interest policy here.

The next question asks about giving bonuses. Make sure to answer this question, no. Nonprofits are not allowed to give bonuses for any reason. This is a key question that the IRS may use to make sure that you understand laws applicable to what you want to do.

Line 7a and b asks about rather you plan to buy items from someone on the board. Unless you are ready to prove why this is the best policy after a long investigation answer this question, no. Continue to answer the questions until the end of this section. The IRS is asking all these questions, because unfortunately too many people try to set up nonprofits to benefit themselves.

You are now ready to move on to the sixth part of Form 1023. The first question asks if you plan to offer services to individuals. Nonprofits can only be organized to benefit classes of people, animals, issues, etc. Therefore, you need to answer this question yes, attach a statement that says that you may choose to give services or funds to individuals affected by our mission. Be specific by stating the mission. Then, continue by giving possible examples. Make sure to state that individuals will be chosen without regard to their sex, religion, or age.

Part 1b is also designed to make sure that you understand the rules. Your nonprofit cannot fundraise and give all the money to another organization. If you plan on helping another organization, then spell it out here in great specifics.

The last question of part six is put here so that the IRS can try to trip up those people who are setting up a nonprofit illegally to compensate another person. You really are answering the same question many times.

The next part asks two simple yes or no questions to determine if you are a new nonprofit. Since you are, you can simply answer no to both questions.

Section eight is one of the longest sections in this long tax form. It is also one of the most important. Therefore, make sure that you take your time and work through it extremely carefully. The first question asks if you support candidates. The answer is no. That is against the law for all types of nonprofits.

There are important issues that may cause your nonprofit to try to influence a legislative question. Therefore, you do not want to close the door to this opportunity at this point. Generally, nonprofits need to spend less than five percent of their donations in this area. As a new nonprofit, simply write a statement that you may try to influence legislative issues at some point in the future, but you have not done so yet. In the event that you do, you will use less than five percent of your nonprofit's time and resources.

The next question asks about Bingo and gaming activities. If you even have any thoughts of holding a legal Bingo game, then make sure to say yes. If you plan on holding a raffle to raise money, then answer yes. Then answer what you expect the nonprofit to earn.

Of course to be a successful nonprofit, you must do fundraising. Check yes to any options that you are considering. This section causes turmoil for many people, but it does not have to be that way. The IRS really doesn't care if you are having a banquet on October 3. Instead, list each activity on a piece of paper and then make a small statement saying broad generalities. For example, you do not anticipate the donation of any cars or boats, but if you receive any donated cars or boats, they will be used to further your mission, or you will be fundraising through the internet including email solutions, a website, and social media.

The next part asks rather you employ professional fundraisers. Most new startups wish that they had this luxury. The next question asks if you have plans to fundraise for another organization. You really need to answer no here. Your focus should be on raising funds for your own nonprofit.

The fourth line of this part which asks about local and national fundraising is another one that causes trouble for some nonprofits. You can simply say that you will engage in fundraising in all 50 states, although your major focus will be on your local market. The reason that you will fundraise in all areas is that you believe there are people across the country who are interested in your mission.

Line 11 in part VIII is also troublesome for some nonprofits. Answer yes and then state that you will accept these donations in accordance with your 501 (c) purpose and that you will determine fair market value based on IRS Publication 561.

The answer to 12 can cause trouble for many organizations that are involved in humanitarian purposes around the globe. If you answer yes, then you need to be very specific about how you will operate. Say that you will seek permits and permission as needed from foreign governments, and that you will comply with sanctions and embargos of the United States government. Then, refer the reader to your narrative to see specifics.

The very next question can also be very trying for some nonprofits. If you do make loans to other organizations, then assure the IRS that you will document these activities. Further, assure the IRS that you will maintain control over how those funds are distributed.

If you said that you would make loans to other nonprofits, then you must be very specific in the next question. Be as specific as possible in this section. If you plan on cooperating with organizations that are better equipped to carry out the field work, then make sure to say that and point out that it helps to fulfill your mission. Further, point out that the nonprofit's board of directors will carry out due diligence in how the funds are spent.

Line 14 asks about foreign organizations. If you plan on working with foreign organizations, you must be extremely specific here. Remember that the idea behind a nonprofit is to raise funds for the nonprofit. Therefore, you really need to be cautious in this area.

Line 14d may be one of the best questions on this entire tax form. This form asks if donors are aware of how their money is being spent. The government wants to make sure that the nonprofit is extremely transparent. All of your donation forms and your website should tell how the money is being spent. Tell the IRS specifically about how you are being a very transparent nonprofit.

In answer part 14 e tell the IRS that you do not make grants to foreign organizations. If your nonprofit chooses to do so in the future, then you will make sure that they are a tax-exempt organization, that you will make sure that they are financially sound, and that they have a great reputation. Additionally, assure the government that you will use all means possible to find out about the organization. For more guidance on this issue see U.S. Department of the Treasury Anti-Terrorist Financing

Guidelines: Voluntary Best Practices for U.S. Based Charities.

The ninth part of Form 1023 asks you to show money that you anticipate coming into the nonprofit and money that you estimate going out of the nonprofit. Now that you have completed the first year's budget, this is actually easy. In order to complete this part, you will need to estimate for the next two years too.

In order to complete the next to last part of Form 1023, the board of directors will need to decide if it is asking to be a Private Foundation and an Operating Private Foundation or a Public Charity. As viewed from the amount of taxes that the nonprofit will owe, it is far better to be seen as a Public Charity. In order to do this, the nonprofit must receive at least 33 percent of its revenue from the public and none from a few select individuals. Of course, the nonprofit must still be involved in one of the qualifying areas such as church, school, hospital or public safety.

Congratulations, the nonprofit has made it to the last part of Form 1023. Now, it is time to pay the applicable fees. As of 2015, the fee to file this form is $400 if you think the nonprofit will not have $10,000 in revenue for any year during the next four years. If the nonprofit anticipates having over $10,000 in revenue for any year during the next four years, then the fee is $800.

The nonprofit has 27 months from the time that it is incorporated to file Form 1023. It is long and cumbersome in many respects. Therefore, it is essential to start early. Along the way, the board of directors will make many important decisions that will guide the nonprofit for many years to come.

CONCLUSION

Forming a nonprofit is a daunting task. If you have gotten to this point, then you deserve to be deeply congratulated. You have shown that you deeply care about your mission and that you are committed to seeing a task through to the end to help other people. You wrote the vision statement and the mission statement so that others could share your vision.

You started the journey, possibly by yourself, by coming up with a project that needed a nonprofit formed. You found that your nonprofit fit one of the 29 types of organizations that qualified to become tax-exempt.

Through your hard work, you found a name for the nonprofit and filled out the right paperwork to have that name trademarked. You brainstormed with others about awesome ideas, narrowed down the list, and worked the process until the job was complete. You then decided the type of trademark that was right for your nonprofit and submitted the paperwork. You worked the process and you succeeded.

Then, you chose your board of directors based on the approach that was right for your nonprofit. You carefully chose men and women who truly had a heart for the mission and were people of character. You then helped them elect officers and form themselves into a proper board.

One of the hardest journeys that you completed was writing the Articles of Incorporation. The nonprofit got the right form from the state and carefully crafted a statement that showed the heart of the nonprofit. You then submitted it and soon discovered that it passed with flying colors, although those may have been anxious days of waiting by the mailbox.

Then, you wrote the Conflict of Interest Policy. This policy gives you great peace of mind, because it means that at no point in time can a director get elected and then take advantage of the money donated to the nonprofit. You hope that that the nonprofit never needs to sanction anyone over this policy, but it feels so good to know that it is in place.

Perhaps the most fun that you had through the entire project, except for the great people you met, was when the nonprofit developed the website. After choosing the right web hosting company and the right design package, you love going to the website and seeing everything that the mission is busy doing, presented all in one location.

The bylaws were actually much easier to craft than you ever imagined possible. While you know that as the nonprofit grows, you will need to visit this area again, it feels so good to have the rules in place. Since it is your sincere hope that the nonprofit lives on into eternity, you wonder how the bylaws will change over time.

Finally, you worked through the process that set the first budget for the nonprofit. You really wonder what wonderful opportunities lie ahead to reach even more people, as donors become more interested in what you are doing. The budget process was rough, but with it you realize that your nonprofit will always remain financially sound.

Finally, you filled out the tax papers that got the nonprofit its tax-exempt status. They were long and complicated, but by handling each part one step at a time, you survived. You have heard so many horror stories, so you are very thankful that you carefully followed each step.

The future looks bright for your nonprofit. The next steps have you even more enthused about the project than you were in the beginning because you have all the groundwork in place to start fundraising and truly helping change the world.

Appendix

This book contains a lot of information. Therefore, as a final thank you gift for downloading this book, we want to give you a checklist that contains important information and the order that you need to complete activities in, to guide you through the process.

Write Vision Statement

Write Mission Statement

Answer what are the needs

Answer what the nonprofit is going to do to meet the needs

Answer beliefs and values that will be used to meet the needs

Decide on the Correct Organizational Type

See list of types on IRS website

Name the Nonprofit

Brainstorm ideas

Choose name that conveys mission

Check internet domain availability

Check U.S. Patent and Trademark Office

File paperwork with state

Claim Internet domain

Trademark name

Choose Board of Directors

Choose correct approach

Choose individuals

Form committees

Elect officers

Write Articles of Incorporation

Get form from state

Fill out form

Send to state with fee

Write Conflict of Interest Policy

Get Form from State if available

Explain conflict of interest to board

Have each board member sign policy

Keep signed copies in safe place

Implement if needed

Create a Website

Choose web hosting company

Choose site layout

Update site regularly

Write Bylaws

Include trademarked name and any "doing business as" names

Spell out powers

List Limitations as required by law

Spell out membership requirements

List meeting requirements

Prepare the Budget

List assets and anticipated revenue including grants, donations from contributors, federated funds, and employee contributions

List expenses including direct costs, program costs, capital costs and overhead costs

Fill Out Form 1023

Obtain Employee Identification Number

List name

Determine fiscal year

List contacts

Give Website

List incorporation date

Provide Articles of Incorporation

Write narrative

List employee and directors compensation

Provide conflict of interest policy

Assure that you are offering services to classes

Properly complete legislative activity

Explain fundraising

Answer questions about foreign organizations

Provide budget

Pay fee

THANK YOU

Thank you again for downloading this book!

I hope this book was able to guide you in starting a nonprofit.

The next step is to stop daydreaming and start a nonprofit. There are so many different areas where nonprofits are needed. Talk to your friends and get busy. After all, the best ideas usually come from people with passions.

Finally, if you enjoyed this book, please take the time to share your thoughts and post a review on Amazon. I really enjoy hearing my readers' feedback and would love to know what you think! You can also check out all of my other books on my Amazon Author Central page

Thank you and good luck on your journey to creating your first Successful Nonprofit!

Made in the USA
Monee, IL
04 February 2020

21282132R20046